Hola Amigo!

By Núria Camahort

To my parents, who gave me everything.

Núria Camahort

Nuria@themagicofamigo.com

www.themagicofamigo.com

Author's Note: This is a work of fiction. Names, characters, places, and incidents are a product of the author's imagination. Locales and public names are sometimes used for atmospheric purposes. Any resemblance to actual people, living or dead, or to businesses, companies, events, institutions, or locales is completely coincidental.

Book design by Castelane.com

Ordering Information: Special discounts are available on quantity purchases by corporations, associations, and others. For details, contact the author at the address above.

First Edition

ISBN 978-1-7347967-0-4

Printed in the United States of America

TO PARENTS AND EDUCATORS:
How to read this book and why

This is a bilingual book to be read ONLY in Spanish. The English notes are just there for you parents, teachers and/or educators to help you engage your children in the story.

But for the kids, this is a Spanish book about who we are and how we feel.

Reading in Spanish is a part of my Immersion methodology with all my students, no matter how young they are, no matter if they have no Spanish background at all.

How to read this book?

This is a book intended to encourage the kids to repeat words and understand their meaning. In each page you will find a short instruction to (using your best sign language) ask the kids to repeat the words and imitate the feelings that the elephant amigo is going through. Short, simple and repetitive language, exaggerated gesture and eye contact help them understand what's going on in the story. When asking the kids to say a new word and fake the feeling, don't go on with the story until they do.

Don't use a word in English. Why?

Immersion is the only natural way to learn a language. Kids learn by listening to the different sounds, processing, understanding their meaning and copying them. It is a subconscious process in which they are not aware of grammatical rules or instructed in any sense. This process is called Language Acquisition. on the other hand, Language Learning is the result of teaching and conscious application of the language rules.

It is scientifically proved that our ability to acquire a new language decreases dramatically after the age of seven. This is one of the reasons why kids do much better than us, adults, and why it is never TOO EARLY to immerse them into the second language.

In addition, kids don't feel ashamed of failing. Have you ever observed how babies learn to walk? They may fall down after trying many times. Do they get ashamed and frustrated? Do they think that they will never walk? More importantly, do they care about anyone looking at them while trying and failing? No. They keep on trying, no fear, no shame. They try until they do and ultimately, they master it! The same happens with language. Kids copy us with no fear of failing. They copy sounds as soon as they hear them.

Let's give them the opportunity to learn other languages in such an easy and painless way!

Núria Camahort

Este es Amigo, un elefante grande, gris y muy simpático. Amigo nos dice "Hola"!

This is Amigo, a big, grey and very nice elephant. Amigo is saying "Hello" to us.

Waive your hands greeting while saying "Hooooolaaaaaa!" in a loud voice.

No oigo "Hola"!

I don't hear "Hello!"

Put your hand behind your ear to emphasize the kids didn't say "Hola" back.

Vamos a decir hola al elefante!

Hooolaaaaa!

Let's say "Hello" to the elephant! Heeeellooooo!

Shake your hands to encourage the kids to say "Hola."

Muy bien!!!

Well done!

Show a thumbs up smiling because the kids said "Hola."

Dice el elefante:

Yo me llamo Amigo. Cómo te llamas tú?

The elephant says, "My name is Amigo. What's your name?"

Point at yourself with two hands. The elephant is saying his name.

Amigo se encuentra con Frío, un oso polar. Le dice:

Yo me llamo Amigo. Cómo te llamas tú?

Amigo finds Frío, a polar bear. He says, "My name is Amigo. What's your name?"

Point at yourself with two hands. The elephant is saying his name.

YO ME LLAMO AMIGO.
CÓMO TE LLAMAS TÚ?

Dice el oso polar:

Yo me llamo Frío.

The polar bear says, "My name is Frío."

Point at yourself with two hands. The polar bear is saying his name.

YO ME LLAMO FRÍO

Amigo y Frío se empiezan a conocer.

Frío le pregunta a Amigo: Cómo estás?

Amigo and Frío greet each other. Frío asks Amigo, "How are you?"

Show the palms of your hands facing up, emphasizing the question "How are you?"

HOLA AMIGO, ¿CÓMO ESTÁS?

Amigo le dice: Yo estoy muy bien!

Amigo says, "I am very well!"

Show a thumbs up.

ESTOY MUY BIEN!

Cuándo estamos muy bien?

Si estoy con mis amigos estoy muy bien!

When do we feel very well? If I am with my friends I feel very well.

Show a thumbs up.

SI YO ENCUENTRO MUCHOS AMIGOS,
YO ESTOY MUY BIEN!

Estoy muy bien!

I am very well!

Encourage the kids to show thumbs up and say "Muy bien."

ESTOY MUY BIEN!

Cuándo estamos tristes?

Si yo estoy solo, estoy muy mal.

When do we feel sad? If I am alone, I feel very bad.

Show thumbs down and sad face. Look around for friends.

Si yo estoy solo, estoy muy mal.

If I am alone, I feel very bad.

Encourage the kids to show thumbs down and sad face, and say "Muy mal."

Si oigo un ruido muy fuerte, "BOOOM"...

Estoy sorprendido!

If I hear a very loud noise, "BOOOM"... I am surprised!

Show fear or surprise, eyes wide open and hands around the face.

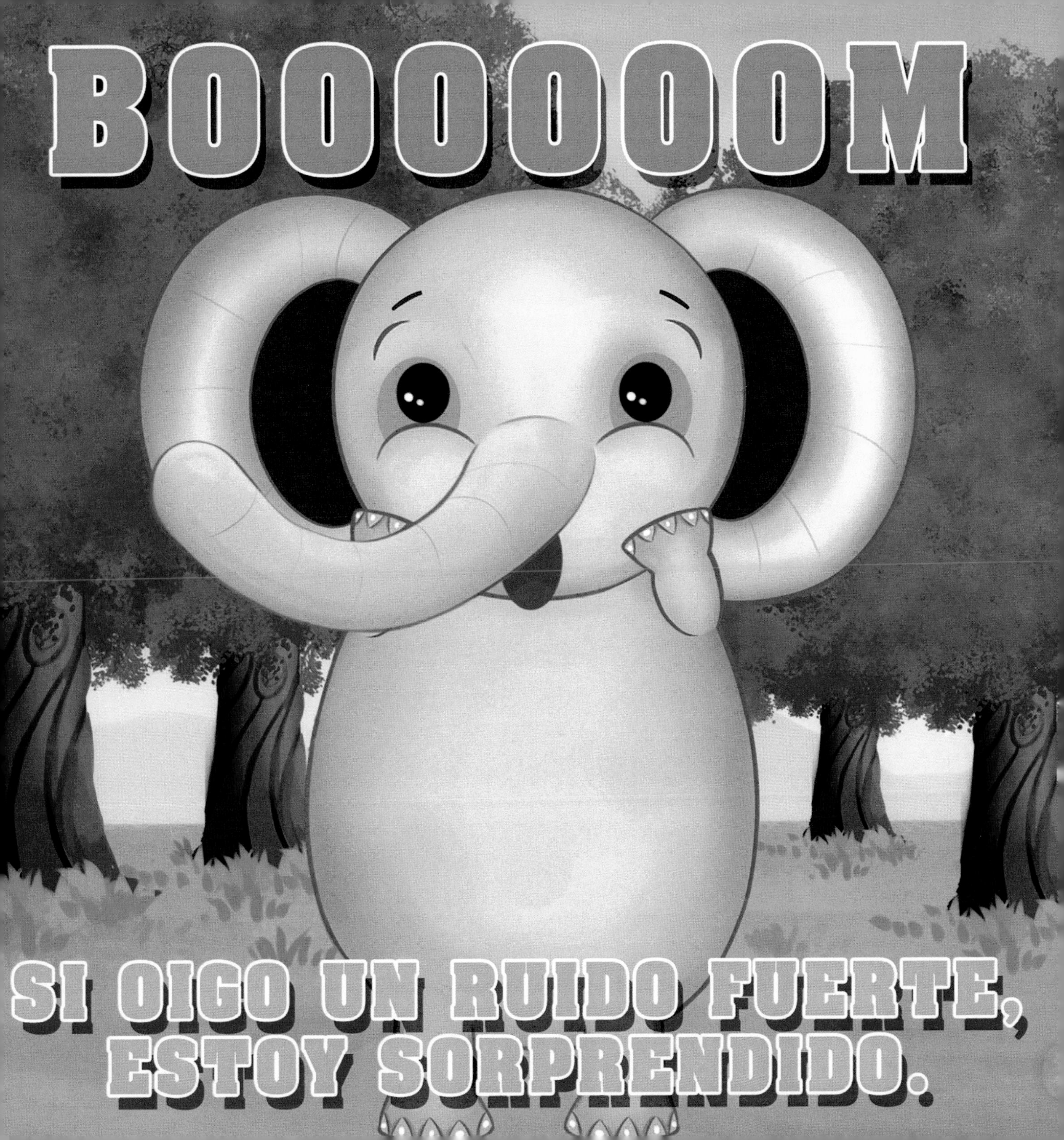

BOOOOOOM

SI OIGO UN RUIDO FUERTE,
ESTOY SORPRENDIDO.

Estoy sorprendido!

I am surprised!

Encourage the kids to copy your expression and say "Sor-pren-di-do."

ESTOY SORPRENDIDO.

Cuándo nos enojamos?

Si mis amigos se esconden, estoy enojado!

When do we get mad? If my friends hide away, I get angry.

Show a mad face, look around and rest a hand on each hip.

SI MIS AMIGOS SE ESCONDEN, YO ESTOY ENOJADO.

Si mis amigos se esconden, estoy enojado!

If my friends hide away, I get mad!

Encourage the kids to copy your expression and say "E-no-ja-do."

Cuándo estamos muy cansados?

Si no duermo de noche, estoy muy cansado.

When do we feel very tired? If I don't sleep at night, I feel very tired.

Show a tired face, eyes half closed and yawn.

SI NO PUEDO DORMIR,
MAÑANA ESTARÉ MUY CANSADO.

Si no puedo dormir, mañana estaré muy cansado.

If I can't sleep, tomorrow I will be very tired.

Encourage the kids to copy your expression and say "Muy cansado."

Cuándo estamos muy felices?

Cuando celebramos un cumpleaños con amigos.

When do we feel very happy? When we celebrate a birthday with friends.

Show a very happy face, hands in the air celebrating.

SI CELEBRO MI CUMPLEAÑOS
ESTOY MUY FELIZ

Si celebro mi cumpleaños, estoy muy feliz!

If I celebrate my birthday, I feel very happy!

Encourage the kids to copy your expression and say "Muy feliz" with loud voices and laugh!

ESTOY MUY FELIIIIIZ

Vamos a repasar!

Muy bien

Muy Mal

Sorprendido　　　　**Muy bien, amigos!**

Enojado

Muy cansado

Muy feliz

Let's go over it again! Very well - Very bad - Surprised - Angry - Very tired - Very happy - Well done my friends!

Encourage the kids to repeat the words of the different feelings showing the right expressions once they do!

Adiós amigos!

Made in the USA
Middletown, DE
04 November 2021